Prison Science: With Special Reference To Recent New York Legislation

Eugene Smith

In the interest of creating a more extensive selection of rare historical book reprints, we have chosen to reproduce this title even though it may possibly have occasional imperfections such as missing and blurred pages, missing text, poor pictures, markings, dark backgrounds and other reproduction issues beyond our control. Because this work is culturally important, we have made it available as a part of our commitment to protecting, preserving and promoting the world's literature. Thank you for your understanding.

ECONOMIC TRACTS. No. XXX.

PRISON SCIENCE

WITH SPECIAL REFERENCE TO

RECENT NEW YORK LEGISLATION

BY

EUGENE SMITH

SECRETARY PRISON ASSOCIATION OF NEW YORK

NEW YORK
THE SOCIETY FOR POLITICAL EDUCATION
330 PEARL STREET
1890

PRISON SCIENCE,

WITH SPECIAL REFERENCE TO RECENT NEW YORK LEGISLATION

PRISON reform has now come to be a department of social science. It was not so in its inception, for the movement toward an improvement in prisons owed its origin entirely to a humane sentiment of pity for the prisoner; it aimed to alleviate the prisoner's sufferings, simply because the cruelties to which he was subjected were needless and revolting; it was a crusade against barbarism, appealing for its support only to the sympathetic instincts of men. But prison reform in its beginning was nothing more than this. It sought to mitigate the prisoner's condition while in prison, but it had no broader reach even with reference to the prisoner himself; it had no conception of a prison *régime* which could, possibly, be made a positive agency in effecting the prisoner's renovation and reform; it did not imagine that the problems it was grappling had any material bearing on the well-being of society at large—much less that those problems involved the interests of the general community primarily, and the interests of the prisoner only secondarily and subordinately. Prison reform, therefore, in its initial stage, was simply negative, destructive; it possessed no constructive principle, no scientific method or claim.

It is interesting to note how this simple humanitarian movement has germinated and expanded until it has evolved modern prison science. The lasting service rendered by John Howard and his compeers was that they awakened public thought concerning prisons and prisoners; their labors enforced the recognition of the convict as a fellow-creature still possessing some of the inalienable rights of manhood and not wholly outside the pale of human sympathy. But this conception involved certain broad corollaries. If the convict has rights as a member of the human family, he is also bound by imperative obligations; reciprocal relations and duties of the convict to society and of society to the convict come into view, and from the study of these relations has been developed the whole science of penology. The old vindictive element of punishment has been wholly extirpated (in theory, though not yet in practice); and it has come to be admitted that the entire penal system of a State rests upon one single principle—*the protection of society*. That principle it is, and that alone, which necessitates and justifies the erection of prisons, the conviction for crime, the imprisonment of offenders; and it is that principle alone that ought to direct and pervade the internal administration of every prison.

The protection of society, however, is a broad aim; it is only partially and temporarily secured by the mere incarceration of the criminal, and it is wholly lost when he is discharged from prison. In order to render the protection effectual and permanent, the convict ought to be subjected to such a disciplinary training in prison as shall tend to rescue him from a life of crime after he regains his freedom. Hence it is that the *reformation* of the criminal not only becomes a legitimate aim, but should be made *the* controlling, paramount aim in the prison regimen. In a political sense, however, the effort made by the State to reform the convict does not rest upon humane or paternal sentiment, seeking to benefit the convict for his own good. The State is not a charitable or missionary agency, and it owes no greater duty to the convict than to other individual members of the community. But reformation is the most radical means of protection: the public weal demands it as a governmental measure best adapted to secure the common safety and promote the general prosperity.

Thus we arrive at the philosophical principle upon which prison reform, which originated in an impulse of Christian charity, has become a political problem, and one of the most important of the public interests with which statesmen and legislators have to deal.

It is no part of the object of this paper to treat of the history of penal legislation, tracing the gradual recognition of the convict's reformation as a possible end to be attained by prison administration. Such a review would yield an utterly inadequate sketch of the real history of prison science, which owes its development to the researches and the experiments of prison managers and inspectors rather than to the efforts of legislators. The laws relating to prisons have, indeed, naturally lagged behind the best thought of the time, and the advance of prison reform has been more often checked than promoted by legislation.

In 1889 the prison laws of New York were revised and codified in a comprehensive act commonly known as the Fassett Law. This law forms an interesting subject of study, because it is above the high-water mark of all previous legislation, on both sides the Atlantic, in the prominence it gives to reformation as an avowed object in the treatment of convicts. It provides a system of prison discipline minute in its details, it embodies many of the most advanced theories of prison science, and it marks, in essential particulars, a new departure in prison legislation. A sufficient time has not yet elapsed since the enactment of this law to afford an experimental demonstration of its merits or its defects, and meantime it offers to the student and to the thoughtful public most inviting topics for reflection.

The most striking feature of this statute is its recognition of the convict's reformation as a controlling aim in prison administration. It is matter of regret that there is no synonym or available substitute in popular use for the term *reformation* as applied to the convict class. The word has a vague latitude of meaning, and is ill-adapted to express the idea it is meant, in this special connection, to signify. There will be found, even among leading writers on reform, a looseness and confusion of thought as to the essential nature of the change in the convict which they designate as his "reformation." And among the public at large the term seems to involve an element that is either unpractical and sentimental or supernatural. There is no room for doubt that imperfect and erroneous conceptions attached to this single word explain much of the popular skepticism about the possibility of reforming convicts on any large scale.

But until the coinage of a new and more exact word, the use of the ambiguous term must be kept within the limits of a rigorous technical definition of its meaning. Reformation, then, in the penological sense, does not imply any religious transformation in the convict; it does not indicate that he must be born again, either morally or intellectually, or even be lifted above the capabilities originally implanted in him. A convict is *reformed* when he has undergone such a change that, being intrusted with freedom, *he will not again commit crime*. This is the sole and entire meaning of reformation as an end sought by the State in its treatment of convicts. The convict, so reformed, may still remain a fit object for religious effort (by the church), for moral training (by society), for humanitarian care and solicitude (by organized benevolence); but when he has become simply and permanently a law-abiding subject, the State has accomplished its whole aim and duty and is done with him. Its jurisdiction reaches no further.

That the drafting of the Fassett Law was done by a master

hand is signally evidenced by the fact that this dubious word "reformation" hardly appears within its four corners. There is found in its stead the following cumbrous, but perfectly lucid, periphrasis: "The reasonable probability that the prisoner will live and remain at liberty without violating the law." This instance fairly illustrates the scientific exactness both of thought and of expression manifested in the whole of this admirable statute.

Thus sharply defined, reformation is resolved into the problem—How to make the convict an obedient subject of the State. This result is not impossible of attainment, as is commonly supposed by those who are unfamiliar with the methods used and with the scientific principles underlying these methods.

The treatment has been evolved from a scientific diagnosis of the criminal character. The popular conception of the criminal type—of that which differentiates the criminal from the common citizen—is radically erroneous. The difference is generally thought to be one of moral *degree* only, the criminal being estimated as simply worse, more devoid of moral principle, than the ordinary citizen. And yet it is true that in our daily walk in life we meet men who are at heart not less dishonest and vicious, not less cruel and brutal, than the most hopeless convicts at Sing Sing; but these men avoid violating the penal code; they do not belong to the criminal class. The real difference between the criminal and the non-criminal is one not of degree, but of *kind* and *quality*. The criminal has got out of relation to the established order of the community in which he lives; he lacks prudential balance, lacks power of self-control; his will is unstable and his whole nature clouded by morbid notions of life.

An actual incident at the Elmira Reformatory, related by Mr. Brockway, illustrates the strange and unhealthy action of the criminal mind. There is a class in the reformatory engaged in the study of practical ethics. The instructor takes up subjects connected with every-day life and treats them in their moral aspects. The most earnest interest has been excited in the class, and free discussion is encouraged. One day the instructor called upon the members of the class to state whether they believed in the common saying that "honesty is the best policy," and, if so, to give reason for their belief. A sharp young prisoner instantly raised his hand, and being accorded permission to answer, set forth the grounds of the faith that was in him somewhat as follows: "I believe that honesty is the best policy from an illustration of it that came within my own knowledge. I knew two brothers, young fellows in New York, who were crooked and dishonest, and they didn't get on well. After a while they went down to Philadelphia and turned over a new leaf. They opened a clothing store there, attended closely to business, were perfectly straight and honest in all their dealings, and they prospered; they enlarged their business and they got the confidence of every one they dealt with. In this way they succeeded in borrowing $100,000. Then they failed, and *they got away with every cent of that money.*"

This was delivered with sober sincerity as convincing evidence to the mind of the speaker of the value of honesty. Another illustration of a similar kind occurred in an examination of this same class. The question was put: "Is it better to beg or to steal?" One prisoner wrote this answer: "A hundred years ago the question presented no difficulty; it would have been better then to beg than to steal. But *now*, when such great progress has been made in prison reform, it would undoubtedly be better to steal than to beg; for the thief being imprisoned would enjoy all the benefits of a reformatory training, which would make him so well able, on his discharge, to take care of himself that he would never afterward have occasion either to beg or to steal."

The intellectual cunning and the moral absurdity of these answers, given in all earnestness, disclose a nature as clearly *askew* as that of a lunatic. They are eminently characteristic of the criminal type. I do not mean to be understood, and I do not believe, that the tendency to crime is a species of lunacy. It is, rather, akin to a moral disease; but it is analogous to lunacy in that it indicates an unhealthy and distorted nature, radically different from the common and normal. I am, of course, speaking broadly. There are many sporadic and exceptional instances where the convict presents no apparently abnormal features; but I am describing the generic characteristics of the criminal class. The criminal, in general, is not animated by the same views, aims, hopes, and motives that commonly direct and restrain human conduct; all is distorted, jaundiced, thoroughly morbid. Morel has happily defined the criminal character as "a morbid deviation from the normal type of humanity." It may denote, according to the atavistic theory of Lombroso, the recurrence of a savage type from the early history of the race before it became civilized; or it may result, according to Maudsley, from an arrested or imperfect development of the individual. The reformation of such a nature is simply a work of *restoration*—a recovery from the morbid to the normal. It largely consists in making the convict to be like other men, by bringing him under the dominion of the same ideas, habits, and motives that everywhere pervade and impel the community, and which are ordinarily sufficient to restrain men from the commission of crime.

Thus, then, we reach a general principle or practical rule, which may be thus formulated: Those methods of prison management are the best calculated to reform the prisoner which assimilate his condition to that of the free workman outside; which cultivate in him the same habits, appeal to the same motives, awaken the same ambitions, develop the same views of life, and subject him to the same temptations that belong to the free community of which he is to be fitted to become a member; and which do all this to the utmost extent compatible with a rigid prison *régime*.

Let not this position be misunderstood. The prison ought to be an abode of hardship and even of wholesome terror. The convict ought to be subjected to a regimen so exacting and rigorous that not only shall it serve a disciplinary purpose, but that he shall carry away an indelible dread of ever again incurring its severities and its disgrace. This dread prevails in every healthy community, and has alone been sufficient to deter many a weak soul from committing crime: it ought to be intensified in the convict. The very first element in a correct prison system is the enforcement of a *hard* discipline; every other consideration must bend to that prime necessity. But the principle on which I am now insisting is that, so far as is consistent with such a discipline, the convict ought to be put in a condition and subjected to motives resembling as closely as possible those that pertain to a free workman outside. In this way he will be best fitted to become a law-abiding member of the community upon his discharge.

This principle furnishes a key for the solution of many problems in prison science. It affords a rule, a gauge, of wider application than any other with which I am acquainted, for testing the merits or defects of prison systems and of measures of penal legislation.

With this criterion in hand, follow the convict on his first entrance into the prison. He finds himself confronted with immediate and pressing wants. He needs (just like any poor honest man) food and clothing and bed. The State is under no obligation to furnish him with any of these things. The public owes no man a living; least of all does the convicted criminal who has defied the laws have any claim on the charities of the State. One thing only the State ought to do, and that obligation arises out of the necessities of the situation. The convict, being deprived of his liberty, cannot get work to do for himself; the State, therefore, ought to provide him with work and pay him proper wages for his labor. The State having done that has in this regard discharged its full duty. And then the condition of the prisoner becomes precisely that of any free laborer—he will have to work for his support; he will have to pay, out of his wages, for whatever he consumes and for the general expenses of his living; and if, by dint of economy and hard work, he is able to earn more than he spends, grant him the privilege, within proper limits, to accumulate his savings until his discharge. Such a fund will then serve a most useful purpose in tiding him over the first trying period when he is adjusting himself to the changed conditions of freedom; or, if he has a family, give him the liberty to apply any possible savings to their support. If he is sick or disabled, the State will provide for him on the humane principle on which it maintains hospitals and asylums. But to the sturdy convict the relation of the State should be that of employer to employee.

Now, mark the natural effects of such a system upon the character of the convict, who was at first an idle vagabond, living on what he could get by depredations. There is necessarily developed in him, in the first place, the *habit* of industry and the habit of self-support by his own labor; he gets used to earning money and to saving money, and to doing both by work; he acquires an experimental knowledge of the value of money and of the value of labor. He becomes accustomed to the idea that industry is the only legitimate means of supplying his wants and of making material progress in life. And when he leaves the prison he comes out a competent and industrious workman, inured to self-support under circumstances so like those on which he now enters as not to suffer any radical shock from altered conditions.

Before inquiring how far the system here described is realized in the New York statute, let us take a glance, by way of contrast, at the old conditions which had until within a few years past prevailed in our State prisons. The convict, on his entrance into the prison, was absolutely relieved of all self-re sponsibility and of nearly all rights. His maintenance was secure —it was the duty of the State to provide that. His labor was hired out to a contractor at so much a head, and all the earnings of his labor belonged solely to the State. We treated our convicts precisely as we treated our cattle: we housed them, fed them, whipped them, worked them, and, to complete the degradation, hired them out by the day; but in the product of labor the convicts themselves had no more interest or right than has the ox that drags the plough. The convict's environment was closely analogous to that of a negro slave under the *régime* of slavery; but it had no counterpart in any free community outside the prison. When the convict was released, he met changed conditions which his imprisonment had positively *unfitted* him to cope with; and the only wonder is that this vicious system did not convert every discharged convict, without a single exception, into a confirmed and irreclaimable criminal. But this old system had one single redeeming feature: it produced one solitary beneficent result: it did serve to develop in the prisoner, perforce, the *habit of industry*. And this habit, so formed, taken in connection with the deterrent dread of being imprisoned again, forms the only explanation I can offer of the really surprising fact that a fraction, estimated above twenty-five per cent., of the convicts treated under the old system did not return to a life of crime.

The New York statute contains recognition of the principle on which such stress has been laid of assimilating the condition of convicts to that of free workmen. It directs that the selection of industries to be carried on in prison shall be made "with reference to employing the prisoners, so far as practicable, in occupations in which they will be likely to obtain employment after their discharge from imprisonment."

It also contains this new and striking provision, that meritorious prisoners may receive compensation in money to an amount not exceeding ten per cent. of the earnings of the prison. Such compensation is to be accumulated and may be drawn upon by the prisoner during his imprisonment, or be applied by the warden "to aid dependent relatives of the prisoner or for books, instruments, or instruction not supplied by the prison;" any balance remaining at the prisoner's discharge is to be subject to his draft. The result of this provision is the same as that of the system I have just advocated, in that it opens to the prisoner the possibility of gaining and saving money; but it differs from it in its vital principle. The allowance made to the prisoner is called "compensation;" but compensation *for* what? Apparently, compensation for *good conduct;* the language of the statute hardly admits of any other answer. Now, however admirable good conduct may be, whether in prison or out of it, where is the free community in which money is earned as a compensation for mere good conduct? And the question may fairly be asked whether it is not a false and hurtful idea to inculcate in the convict that he ought to be paid money for simply conducting himself well. It is labor, and labor only, that earns and is fairly entitled to pecuniary compensation. A reward for good conduct, by whatever name it may be called, is a gratuity, given of grace and not a compensation, earned of right. Thus the Fassett Law fails to secure by this provision any of the wholesome disciplinary benefits which have been pointed out as likely to accrue from a system where the convict receives wages for his labor and incurs the necessity of self-support. Instead, the law presents the rather demoralizing notion that good conduct may be paid for in money. It leaves untouched and in full force the old theory that it is the duty of the State to grant free maintenance to its prisoners—a theory which pauperizes the convicts and is utterly indefensible on any logical ground—and the product of prison industry still remains under the law the absolute property of the State.

It is only just to state, once for all, that any adverse criticism upon the New York statute implies no reflection upon the intelligence or skill of the composer of that statute. It must not be forgotten that the Fassett Bill was enacted under the stress of hostile and clashing interests. Every clause of it was subjected to jealous scrutiny by representatives of the labor unions and of factions opposed to all prison labor. It was passed by a legislature where influences adverse to an enlightened system of prison labor and discipline were not perhaps controlling, but potent. Any measure that met the united and determined opposition of the labor party was practically doomed to defeat. Had the bill defined the proper relation of the State to its convicts as analogous to that of an employer to his employees, or placed the convict on the footing of a workman receiving wages, it could not possibly have been enacted. Such a proposition would have created as wild a turmoil in the labor party as would have been caused forty years ago in a slaveholders' convention by the proposal to liberate the slaves. The Fassett Bill was the best attainable compromise, and the provision regarding compensation for good conduct was the nearest feasible approach to an ideally correct system. It is only matter of wondering gratitude that a law containing so many advanced and beneficent provisions and so few positively objectionable features was actually passed by a large majority of votes.

One very vital point on which the advocates of the new law encountered strenuous opposition related to the use of machinery in carrying on prison industries. A bill to abolish the use of machinery in prisons is an annually-recurring measure in the New York Legislature, and it has required the most vigilant efforts of the friends of prison reform to prevent its enactment. The industries practised in prison ought to be the same as those prevailing outside, and they ought to be carried on by the same methods. Machinery having supplanted hand-work in the workshops of the world, the convict must be trained in the use of machinery for precisely the same reason that the free workman must be. If trades exceptional and little followed outside are introduced in prison, or if obsolete or unusual methods of work are employed, the convict will not be qualified by his prison training (as he ought to be) to earn a living on his discharge. The opposition to the use of machinery in the prisons proceeds, of course, from the labor unions, which by their strikes and boycotts and their rigorous internal organization have gained an iron grip on all the labor of the country, except prison labor. In their efforts to curtail and cripple that, the labor unions lose sight of or are unmoved by the fact that their schemes, if successful, would cruelly deprive the discharged convict of the possibility of earning an honest livelihood, and would force him back to a life of crime. The Fassett Law triumphantly secured the use of machinery in prison labor; and it is believed that the policy thus enacted, which is absolutely indispensable for the attainment of any permanent reformative results, is not likely to be reversed in the future legislation of New York.

The New York statute must also be tested by the application of another fundamental principle of prison science. This may be called the principle of "individual treatment of convicts." Nothing is more certain than that the inmates of a prison can never be reformed *en masse* by the application of a uniform, unvarying method. As well might the patients in a general hospital, afflicted with divers diseases, be all cured by one universal and unbending regimen. Each case is different from all the rest, and demands a separate care and treatment. It is true that the prison must be administered under a uniform system of rules and regulations, binding all the prisoners alike; and here lies the danger of institutionalism. But God's government of the world proceeds under laws, physical and moral, that are universal and absolutely inflexible; and yet there remains the widest play for individuality, and we believe that the development of every human life progresses under the guidance of a special divine providence. There must preside over every prison a supervising intelligence that thoroughly knows each prisoner; that is capable of gauging each prisoner's capacity, of detecting his special adaptabilities and weaknesses, of testing his moral strength, of measuring his progress; an intelligence that is ever striving to find in each prisoner his latent spark of manhood, and, when found, to fan it into life. There is no calling in life that demands a more astute knowledge of human nature, or that opens to such knowledge a wider field of beneficence, than the position of governor of a prison. No system however judicious, no legislation however wise, can insure a successful prison *régime*. To attain that, the whole administration must be pervaded by the *personality* of a warden who shall possess keen insight, broad human sympathies, and a strong and masterful nature; and that personality must be brought into separate and direct contact with each prisoner. A correct prison system should serve to unfold and disclose the distinctive character of each prisoner, so that his case may be open to diagnosis and to separate treatment.

This vital principle of prison science finds abundant recognition in the New York statute. That law embodies numerous provisions, the aim of which is to secure and preserve the fullest information regarding the history, environment, character, and progress of every prisoner. Beginning at the time of the prisoner's conviction, it is made the duty of the court to ascertain by examination of the convict, and by such other evidence as can be obtained, whether such convict has learned and practised any mechanical trade, and any other facts tending to indicate the causes of his criminal character or conduct. A certificate of the facts thus obtained is transmitted to the warden of the prison where the convict is confined. It furnishes a basis on which the warden is required to classify the convicts. Three classes or grades are provided for: in the first are those convicts who are least vicious and give hopeful promise of reform; in the second, those of a lower moral order, while the third includes the hopelessly incorrigible. The classification made in the first instance must be largely tentative, but the classes are always open to readjustment, and prisoners may be degraded or promoted from one grade to another. The classes are to be kept apart from each other and to be subjected to separate treatment.

A minute record is to be kept, showing the standing of each prisoner in demeanor, in education, and in labor during the whole term of his confinement. The chaplain and physician are required to make full and constant reports to the warden of the condition of the convicts and of the progress made by them. Education, industrial, mental, and moral, is made compulsory. All these provisions are most admirable. The life of each convict proceeds under a searching supervision, which tests his capacities in every direction; his strength and his weakness become inevitably revealed to the watchful eye of a competent warden. Shams and deception can hardly be sustained under proofs so varied and constant. Thus the character of each convict comes to be intimately known; his power of self-control, his strength of purpose, the degree to which he can be trusted, the measure of progress he is making, can be computed and tested; and a reasonable estimate can be formed of his qualifications for a life of freedom.

And thus we are brought to the special and crowning features of the New York statute—*the indeterminate sentence* and the conditional liberation on parole.

The act provides that when any male person over sixteen years of age shall be convicted of felony, the court may pronounce a sentence without fixing the term of imprisonment, except that the imprisonment shall not be shorter than the minimum term nor longer than the maximum term for which the convict might have been sentenced.

The indeterminate sentence is the logical sequence of the

modern theory of imprisonment. Under the old theory of retribution the convict was to be *punished*, made to suffer, as an expiation of his crime. That theory demanded that the term of imprisonment should be made longer or shorter, according to the greater or lesser enormity of the crime. Hence in every case of conviction the judge was required to make a mental computation of the exact degree of the prisoner's criminality, and to fix the term of imprisonment accordingly in pronouncing sentence. The result was, necessarily, in most cases, gross injustice. The judge had no data on which to form an intelligent judgment of the degree of the prisoner's guilt; he was called upon to solve a most complex psychological problem, depending on the prisoner's environment and training, on the prisoner's strength of mind and power of moral perception, on the attendant circumstances tending to palliate or aggravate the crime; and on all these questions the judge was compelled to rely largely on his imagination or his unenlightened sympathies. Misleading incidents at the trial, the individual temper of the judge, a haphazard guess, determined the length of the sentence—one year—five years—twenty years. The miscarriage of justice thus often resulting, with the chance of an unduly light sentence, has cast disrepute upon the administration of the law; it has created among the criminal class a widespread belief that judicial sentences are unjust and not impartial. Let me give an instance. Here is an extract from the Hartford *Courant*, giving the report of a day's proceedings in a criminal court. Observe the disparity of the sentences pronounced; and although possibly the punishment may in each case have accurately fitted the crime, estimate the demoralizing effect of this report upon a criminal reader:

The criminal court "resumed business yesterday morning and took up the cases of Edward Garland and James Allen. . . . Each pleaded guilty to a second count on a principal charge of burglary, and Garland was sentenced to jail for nine months and Allen for two months.

"William Jett pleaded guilty to statutory burglary and was sentenced to six months in jail.

"Joseph Scott, charged with stealing from the person, pleaded guilty to a third offence of theft and was sent to jail for four months.

"John Doyle pleaded not guilty to the theft of a watch, was tried, found guilty by the jury, and sentenced to jail for three months and fined $5 and costs.

"Dr. John Young, charged with the theft of a gold watch, was found guilty by the jury and sentenced to State prison for three years."

The injustice and illogical absurdity of requiring the court to fix in advance the term of the convict's confinement are made vastly more glaring in the light of the modern theory of imprisonment. Under this theory the confinement of the convict is not an act of vengeance, but simply a measure of defence to the community. The convict is put in prison on the same principle that a yellow-fever ship is kept in quarantine or a small-pox patient confined in an hospital. The conviction for crime is an adjudication that the offender is dangerous to society, and that the public security requires that he should not be allowed to go at large; for that reason, and for that reason alone, the State shuts him up in a prison. What, now, can be more illogical than to prescribe in advance *how long* his imprisonment shall continue? The same reason of public safety that exacts his imprisonment in the first instance demands that he shall not be released until it becomes safe that he should be set free. It is just as irrational to send a lunatic to an insane asylum for the predetermined period of two years as it is to sentence a felon to two years' imprisonment, decreeing in advance that when the two years are up both shall go scot free. Both should be confined until they have become so far *cured* that they may be set at large without danger to the community. How long such confinement should last no human intelligence can foretell; it may be one year—it may be for life.

Logically, therefore, a sentence of imprisonment which is absolutely indeterminate as to its duration is the only defensible one. Practically, however, there are some important considerations that call for caution before adopting the system without restriction. The indeterminate sentence presupposes two things, which are conditions precedent to its just operation: first, that the prison treatment shall be such as tends to cure the criminal tendency; and, second, that there shall be a means of determining when the cure has been effected.

The indeterminate sentence is part of a complex system of reform. The State is unjust if it throws the convict into a prison where all the influences surrounding him are vicious and demoralizing, and then demands that he reform himself as the condition of his release. If the State exacts such terms of freedom, it is bound to environ the prisoner with conditions that render reformation possible; it must check the contagion of vice that comes from unrestrained companionship; it must subject the prisoner to salutary discipline; it must educate his mind and heart and conscience; it must occupy his time and thought with duties that are elevating and strengthening; it must apply to him all those curative influences which modern prison science has devised in the treatment of crime. If the convict resist all these therapeutic agencies, then he is incorrigible; and while he is incorrigible, he has the right to live, but he has no right to live at large, nor has the State the right to set him free.

These reformative methods it is the aim of the New York statute to introduce and put into practical, effective operation in the prisons of the State. But the departure is a new and revolutionary one. The methods of treatment heretofore practised in the penitentiaries and State prisons have not been reformative; they have not uplifted the convict, but have cast him down; they have made the ex-convict not a law-abiding citizen, but the most direful terror and scourge to the community. The new methods of reform must be of slow growth and development; they cannot be introduced and put into successful operation within a year or within five years. They must be slowly elaborated and tested by the intelligent zeal of the prison wardens. Not the legislators, but the wardens, control the practical destinies of prison reform; and all that legislation can accomplish is to mark out a system, the actual administration of which in any prison is dependent, for success or for failure, upon the ability and good faith of its executive managers.

It may be assumed that the actual managers of the prisons of New York will endeavor with cordial sympathy to carry into effect the spirit of the new law; but if they do so the present is a period of laborious transition from the old to the new which must continue for many years. If the new system of reformative training indicated by the New York statute shall become firmly established and in successful working by the close of the present century, the rate of growth will be quite as rapid as it is reasonable to expect. Now, in the mean time, until the prison discipline of the State shall have become actually reformative in its results, the indeterminate sentence, as a part of that discipline, must be used tentatively and with some caution. Were it enforced now with logical rigor, it would be apt to work disastrously, in the absence of a really reformatory discipline, which is its necessary complement. It would congest the prisons of the State, inasmuch as commitments would continue while discharges would cease. Until the State can positively reform its convicts and thus provide a practicable outlet from the prisons, the indeterminate sentence cannot safely be applied without some restriction. For these reasons the New York statute proceeds with wisdom, I think, in adopting the indeterminate sentence with certain cautious qualifications. It provides that the courts *may* pronounce such sentence; the exercise of the authority is discretionary, not compulsory. The confinement of the sentence between minimum and maximum limits is wholly illogical, but it marks a sound tentative policy. There will be time enough to efface these limits when the reformative system shall have been more broadly developed.

For the same reasons I am disposed not to condemn another feature of the statute which is logically incompatible with the indeterminate sentence. I refer to the section which retains in full force the power of the governor of the State to pardon. Under an ideal reformatory system the operation of the indeterminate sentence should never suffer encroachment by an executive pardon. The prisoner will be released whenever he becomes fit for freedom, and there ought to be no power in the governor to set him free at any earlier period. But when the ideal system shall have become the actual system, it will be soon enough to stop any possible exercise of executive clemency. Meantime it is better to sin against logic than to suffer a possible miscarriage of justice.

Those provisions of the New York statute which regulate the *labor* of the prisoners are the ones that will excite the widest interest; for prison industry, besides being the most vital concern of prison science, is a very important interest in political economy.

In treating this branch of the statute, it may be stated, first, in general terms, that the law retains the entire abolition of the contract system, and adopts both the public-account and the piece-price plans, with a preference for the public-account system. It limits to 100 the number of prisoners that shall be employed in each of the three specified industries of manufacturing stoves, iron hollow ware, and boots and shoes, and provides generally that the total number of prisoners to be employed in manufacturing any one kind of goods shall not exceed five per cent. of the number of all those employed within the State in manufacturing the same kind of goods. These restrictions, although in fact a concession to the labor party, are defensible on sound principles. A large diversity of employments gives wider scope to the individual treatment of convicts and enlarges the opportunity to develop special aptitudes. It also avoids the stigmatizing of any particular lines of manufacture as distinctively "prison" industries.

The novel features of the statute are those which adjust the labor with reference to the classification of the convicts. The three grades into which the prisoners are to be divided have been already mentioned.

The first grade is composed of those who give fair promise of reform, and the statute enacts that their labor shall be directed "with reference to fitting the prisoner to maintain himself by honest industry after his discharge, as the primary or sole object of such labor." The first-grade prisoners may be employed at "labor for industrial training and instruction solely, even though no useful or salable products result from their labor."

The second grade is composed of those prisoners who appear to be incorrigible but are competent to work and reasonably obedient to prison discipline. Their labor shall be directed primarily to the production of salable goods, and secondarily to fitting them for a life of self-support after their discharge.

The third grade comprises those prisoners who appear to be incorrigible or so insubordinate or incompetent as to seriously interfere with the discipline of the prison. Their labor shall be directed solely to such exercise as shall tend to the preservation of health, or to manufacturing without machinery such articles as are needed in the public institutions of the State, or to other manual labor which shall not compete with free labor.

The scheme of the statute regarding labor is novel and simple; it turns on the distinction between the corrigible and the incorrigible prisoners. For those who are amenable to reformative influences, the primary controlling aim is to fit them for a life of honest self-support; for those who are irreclaimably vicious, the object of their labor is to be simply the production of salable goods. This method of adjusting convict labor is based upon perfectly sound principles. Where there is a reasonable prospect of reclaiming a criminal, his labor and all the other agencies of prison discipline ought to be concentrated to effect his rehabilitation. But where the convict proves irresponsive to all reforming influences and hopelessly vicious, it is just that he should be made to labor for production only, and thus to contribute, as far as possible, to the payment of the expense with which his crime has burdened the State.

One criticism only I have to offer upon this branch of the statute. The convict, on his first entrance into the prison, may appear to the warden to be incorrigible, and may be placed at once in the second or third grade; and there he may remain until he shall have served out the maximum term of his sentence. He would then be discharged *without ever having been subjected to a reformatory course of treatment.* Every convict ought to undergo the test of a thorough reformatory discipline; until that test has been faithfully applied and has failed, no convict ought to be adjudged incorrigible and treated as one without hope. The statute condemns a convict as incorrigible on his first commitment if he appear such to the warden. No convict ought to be classed an incorrigible on mere appearances. Subject every prisoner to healthful and life-giving influences, and not until he has resisted every beneficent test should he be given over to despair.

This objection, however, is one that relates practically to the execution of the law, and can be met by a vigilant administration. The statute, viewed as a whole, is a broad, philosophical act of legislation, offering a free scope for the application of most advanced principles of prison science and marking a very long stride of progress. And it is the act of the Legislature of New York, which has thus made itself the leader in reform! The New York Legislature is a body which is itself classed as incorrigible in popular estimation. It is possible that this may be an instance where the appearance of incorrigibility is deceptive. While such a grand and beneficent statute stands as the enactment of the Legislature of New York, it is not yet time to despair of the cause of prison reform.

The Society for Political Education.

PUBLICATIONS.

The Society issues for its members not fewer than four tracts in each year upon subjects selected by the Committee. The following tracts have been issued, and any not noted as out of print may be had from the Secretary. Subscribers for 1890 are entitled to tracts beginning with No. 27.

ECONOMIC TRACTS.

1. ATKINSON (E.). What is a Bank? 10 cents. (Out of print.)
2. POLITICAL ECONOMY AND POLITICAL SCIENCE. A priced and classified bibliography by Sumner, Wells, Foster, Dugdale, and Putnam. 25 cents.
   (*This tract, carefully revised and extended, will be republished at an early date.*)
3. PRESENT POLITICAL AND ECONOMIC ISSUES, with suggestions of subjects for debate and for essays. 25 cents. (Out of print.)
   (*This tract has been reissued as No. 28 in enlarged form.*)
4. THE USURY QUESTION, by Calvin, Bentham, Dana, and Wells, with bibliography. 25 cents.
5. COURTOIS (Alphonse). Political Economy in One Lesson. Translated by W. C. Ford. 10 cents.
6. WHITE (Horace). Money and Its Substitutes. 25 cents.
7. WHITE (A. D.). Paper-Money Inflation in France: a History and Its Application. 25 cents.
8. WHITRIDGE (Frederick W.). The Caucus System. 10 cents.
9. CANFIELD (James H.). Taxation. 15 cents.
10. BOWKER (R. R.). Of Work and Wealth; a Summary of Economics. 25 cents.
11. GREEN (George Walton). Repudiation. 20 cents.
12. SHEPARD (E. M.). The Work of a Social Teacher; Memorial of Richard L. Dugdale. 10 cents.
13. FORD (W. C.). The Standard Silver Dollar and the Coinage Law of 1878. 20 cents.
14. SHEPARD (Edwd. M.). The Competitive Test and the Civil Service of States and Cities. 25 cents.
15. RICHARDSON (H. W.). The Standard Dollar. 25 cents.
16. GIFFEN (Robert). The Progress of the Working Classes in the Last Half Century. 25 cents.
17. FOSTER (W. E.). References to the History of Presidential Administrations—1789–1885. 25 cents.
18. HALL (C. H.). Patriotism and National Defence. 15 cents.
19. ATKINSON (E.). The Railway, the Farmer, and the Public. 15 cents.
20. WEEKS (Jos. D.). Labor Differences and Their Settlement. 25 cents.
21. BOWKER (R. R.). Primer for Political Education. 15 cents.
22. BOWKER (R. R.). Civil Service Examinations. 15 cents.
23. BAYLES (J. C.). The Shop Council. 15 cents.
24. WILLIAMS (Talcott). Labor a Hundred Years Ago. 15 cents.
25. Electoral Reform, with the Massachusetts Ballot Reform Act, and New York (Saxton) Bill. 15 cents.
26. ILES (George). The Liquor Question in Politics. 15 cents.
27. A REVISED AND EXTENDED REISSUE OF No. 2. In preparation. 25 cents.
28. QUESTIONS FOR DEBATE IN POLITICS AND ECONOMICS, with a Form of Constitution and By-laws for Debating Clubs. 25 cents.
29. FOSTER (William E.). References on the Constitution of the United States: its Sources, Commentaries, and Interpretations. 25 cents.
30. SMITH (Eugene). Prison Science, with Special Reference to Recent New York Legislation. 10 cents.

GEORGE ILES, Secretary,
330 Pearl St., New York.

THE SOCIETY FOR POLITICAL EDUCATION.

EXECUTIVE COMMITTEE.

R. R. BOWKER, New York, *Chairman.*
E. M. SHEPARD, New York, *Treasurer.*
GEORGE ILES, New York, *Secretary.*
WORTHINGTON C. FORD, Washington, D. C.
WILLIAM M. IVINS, New York.
GEORGE HAVEN PUTNAM, New York.
A. E. WALRADT, New York.
DAVID A. WELLS, Norwich, Conn.

ADVISORY COMMITTEE.

JOHN H. AMES, Lincoln, Neb.
E. D. BARBOUR, Boston, Mass.
A. SYDNEY BIDDLE, Philadelphia, Pa.
GEORGE S. COE, New York.
B. R. FORMAN, New Orleans, La.
GEN. BRADLEY T. JOHNSON, Baltimore, Md.
RICHARD W. KNOTT, Louisville, Ky.
FRANKLIN MACVEAGH, Chicago, Ill.
HORACE RUBLEE, Milwaukee, Wis.
M. L. SCUDDER, JR., Chicago, Ill.
EDWIN BURRITT SMITH, Chicago, Ill.
ANDREW D. WHITE, Ithaca, N. Y.
HORACE WHITE, NEW YORK.
F. W. ZEILE, San Francisco, Cal.

OFFICE ADDPESS: 330 PEARL STREET, NEW YORK.

Printed by Libri Plureos GmbH in Hamburg, Germany